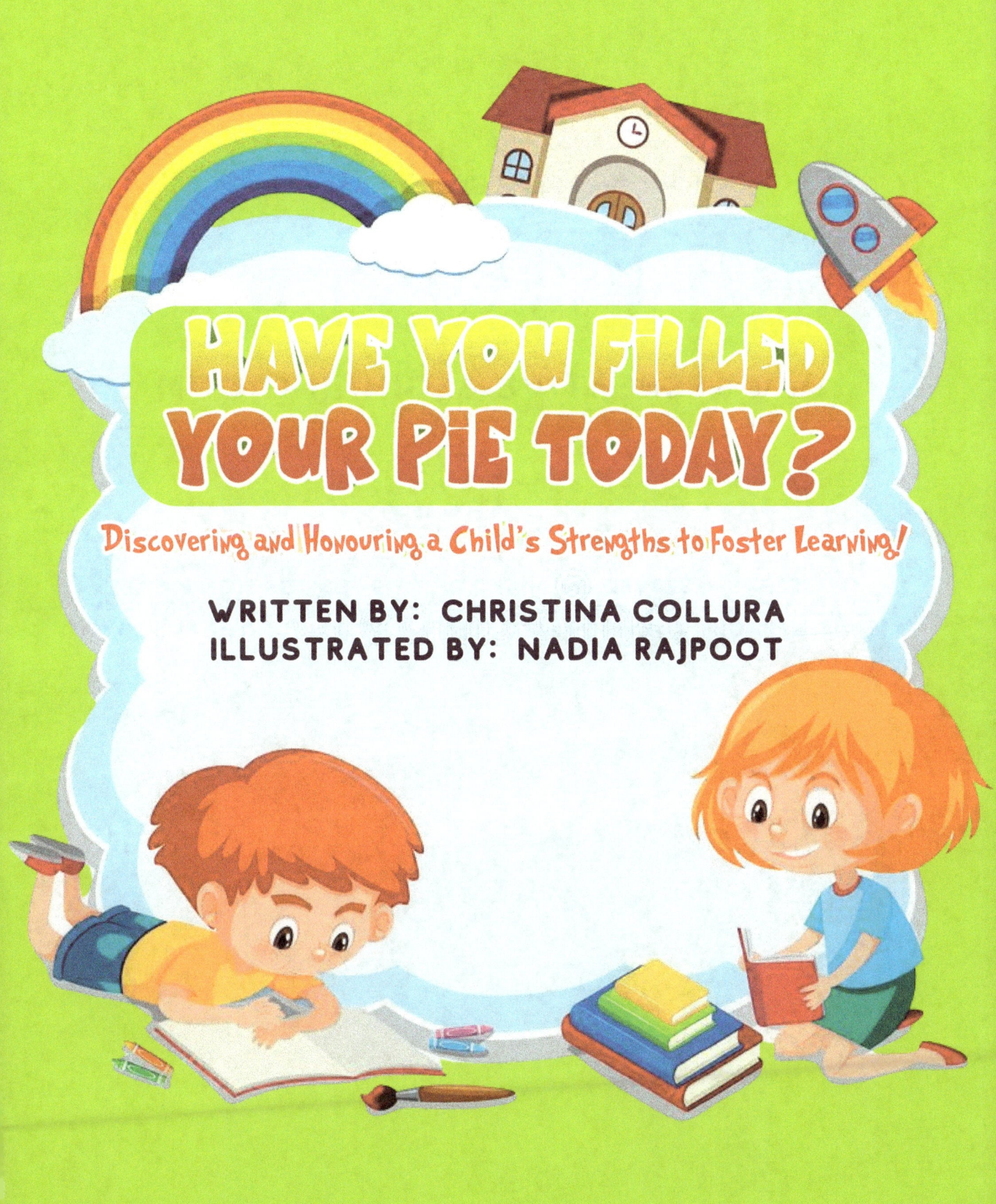

Copyright @ 2023 Creative Beginning

WWW.CREATIVE-BEGINNING.COM

ALL RIGHTS RESERVED. NO PART OF THIS PUBLICATION MAY BE REPRODUCED, TRANSMITTED, OR STORED IN ANY FORM OR BY ANY MEANS WITHOUT THE PRIOR WRITTEN PERMISSION OF THE PUBLISHER

This book is dedicated to:
All the incredible children who teach the individuals around them the amazing skills they have; teaching us everyday about their learning journey!

"Good morning, friends!" Ms. Cook said as she greeted her students' as they arrived in the classroom.

"Please join me on the carpet" she told her students' as they were hanging up their hats and backpacks.

"How was your weekend?" Ms. Cook asked. Students' began to put their hands up and share what they did on the weekend.

Luca excitedly rocked on his wobbly cushion and yelled out "I PLAY PARK, I PLAY PARK!".

Ms. Cook waited for a moment for Luca to calm down before showing him how to "put up his hand".

"I am so happy you shared Luca! Hope you had fun playing at the park!". Ms. Cook replied with a smile.

The students' listened intently while Ms. Cook began sharing a story. Luca sat wobbling on his cushion, while holding his favourite fidget toy to keep his hands busy.

After the story, Ms. Cook told her students' they were going to be working with numbers at their tables.

Ms. Cook smiled and replied "We are going to be working with our numbers! Take a peek at our centres and see which one you would like to work at." The students' peered at the activities that were on the classroom tables.

"I would like to use the big numbers and cubes," said Victoria.

"I would like to use my pencil to write today!" said David.

"I had a feeling you would say that, David!" Ms. Cook said with a smile. "How would you like to work on your numbers today, Matthew?" she asked.

"I would like to work on the IPAD today!" he said.

What the students' didn't know was that Ms. Cook had already been learning all about the ways her students' liked to learn.

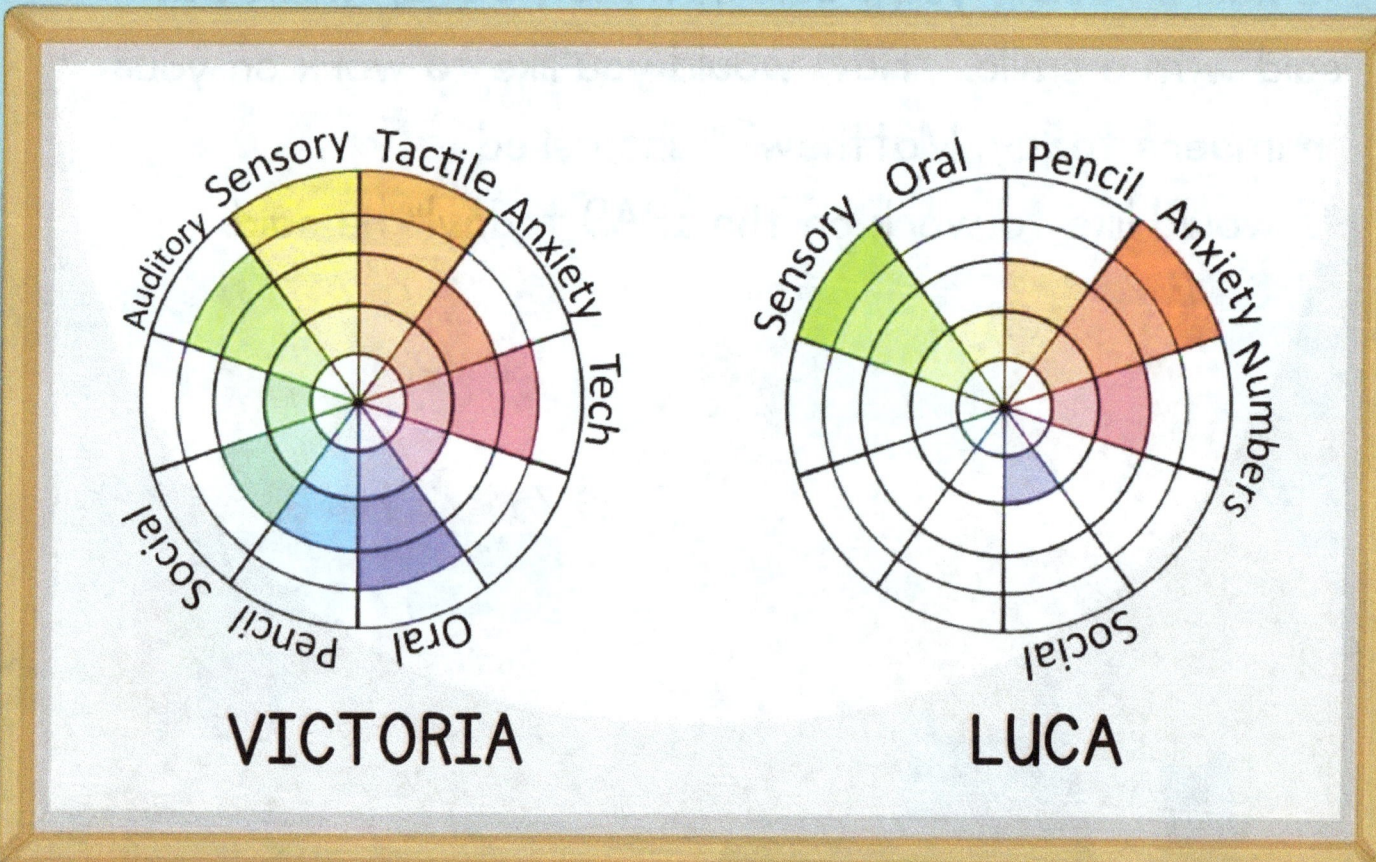

VICTORIA

LUCA

This was important as she began to realize that every child may be learning the same skill, but they all learn in DIFFERENT ways!

Luca likes using chalk. She thinks he really likes the texture! Ms. Cook sat Luca down at a table with his Chalkboard-Based Number Puzzle and watched the magic happen!

You could tell by the excitement on his face that he enjoyed writing in the spaces with the chalk and telling Ms. Cook what number he printed in the spaces!

Ms. Cook observed her students' and walked around to listen and see the learning happening.

She was so happy to see that she had chosen activities to help build on her students' strengths and interests. After a short time, she welcomed them back to the carpet again.

Great job friends! Please join me on the carpet again!

Victoria put her hand up and still asked in wonder "How does working with numbers fill our pie?" "Well.... we all have different ways of learning and when you play and learn the way you like or feel comfortable, you are filling your PIE!" she explained.

"Victoria liked to play with big numbers and cubes, David liked to work with a pencil and paper, Matthew liked to play with the IPAD and Luca liked using chalk. Plus...you were all learning about reading and writing numbers! Pretty cool right?" she continued.

How does working with numbers fill our pie?

"So sneaky Ms. Cook!" laughed Matthew

"Thank you for teaching and showing me how to fill your pie today and everyday!" smiled Ms. Cook.

"Autism Is Not Linear"

www.creative-beginning.com

About the Author

Christina Collura is an Elementary School Teacher in Toronto, Ontario, as well as the Founder and CEO of Creative Beginning - home to an incredible Chalkboard- Based Puzzle Line. She continues to use her platform to advocate for children of ALL needs and abilities! Christina firmly believes that identifying a child's strengths (regardless of a diagnosis) and how they need to learn is vital to a child's successful learning path!

This is Luca! Luca was diagnosed with Autism at the age of 3! In that moment, we knew his learning wasn't going to be a barrier, but a learning curve for those who he came in contact with! Luca learned to write his name with a Chalkboard- Based Puzzle created by his mom (Christina Collura), which lead to a whole line of Chalkboard-Based products that are benefiting and bridging the gap between children of ALL needs and abilities!

For more information about our Award Winning Chalkboard -Based Puzzles; please visit: www.creative-beginning.com

www.ingramcontent.com/pod-product-compliance
Lightning Source LLC
Chambersburg PA
CBHW081238080526
44587CB00022B/3990